£7.99

we love you...

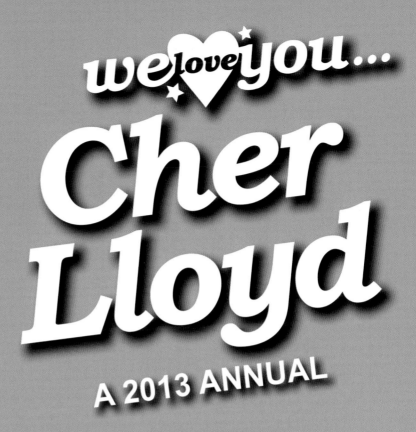

we ♥ love you...
Cher Lloyd

A 2013 ANNUAL

Written by Chas Newkey-Burden
Designed by Jane Greig

PBR

A Pillar Box Red Publication

ISBN: 978-1-907823-32-9

Contents

Cher's Early Days

Cher has lived the dream of many, enjoying show business success in Britain and America. She is one of our most famous pop celebrities but she has never forgotten where it all started.

She was born on July 28, 1993, and grew up in Worcester. Her family lived in a red-brick terraced council house in a rough part of Malvern, a spa town. She later attended the Chase School in Malvern and went on to study performing arts at Dyson Perrins College as her musical ambitions formed. She also took classes at the theatre arts school Stagecoach.

Back at home, Cher could often be found dreaming of what she could achieve as a pop star. As she watched established artists on television she wondered if she could ever follow in their footsteps. She learned to rap by chanting along to instrumental tracks on YouTube. Her three siblings soon grew familiar with the sound of her rapping and singing in her bedroom. They were impressed by what they heard. In 2008 she was named best solo female at Worcestershire's Pop Idol competition.

However, outside the warm surroundings of her family home, life was often hard for Cher

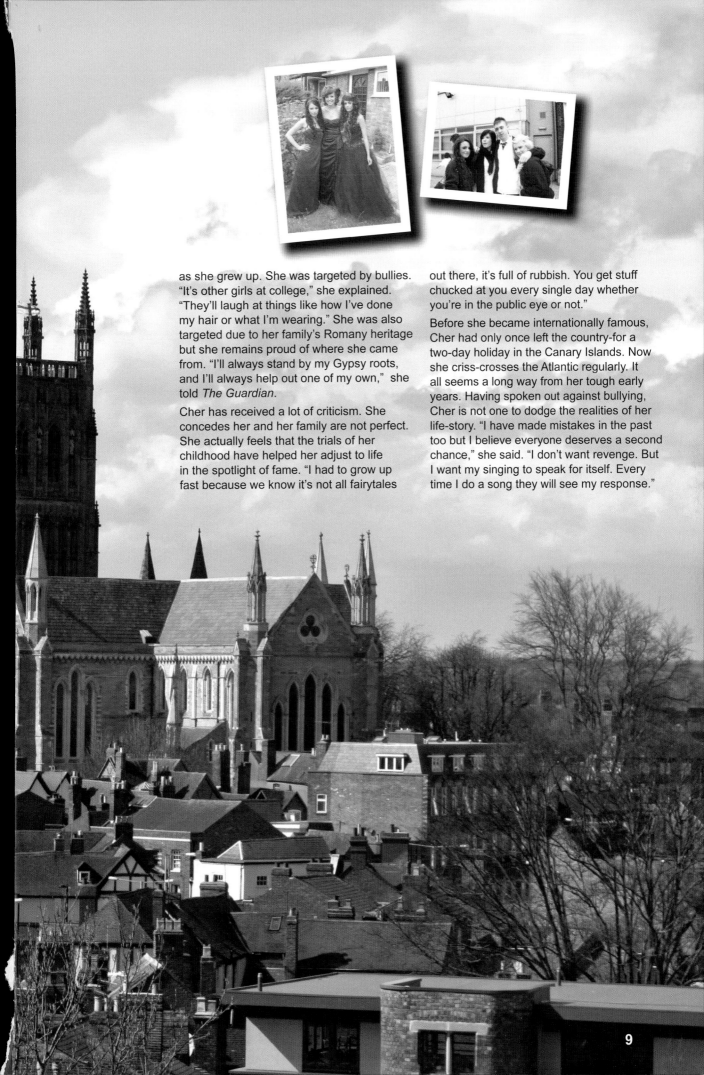

as she grew up. She was targeted by bullies. "It's other girls at college," she explained. "They'll laugh at things like how I've done my hair or what I'm wearing." She was also targeted due to her family's Romany heritage but she remains proud of where she came from. "I'll always stand by my Gypsy roots, and I'll always help out one of my own," she told *The Guardian*.

Cher has received a lot of criticism. She concedes her and her family are not perfect. She actually feels that the trials of her childhood have helped her adjust to life in the spotlight of fame. "I had to grow up fast because we know it's not all fairytales out there, it's full of rubbish. You get stuff chucked at you every single day whether you're in the public eye or not."

Before she became internationally famous, Cher had only once left the country-for a two-day holiday in the Canary Islands. Now she criss-crosses the Atlantic regularly. It all seems a long way from her tough early years. Having spoken out against bullying, Cher is not one to dodge the realities of her life-story. "I have made mistakes in the past too but I believe everyone deserves a second chance," she said. "I don't want revenge. But I want my singing to speak for itself. Every time I do a song they will see my response."

we love you...

10

we love you...

Wordsearch

Can you find the following Cher Lloyd related words hidden in the wordsearch below? Words can go horizontally, vertically and diagonally in all eight directions. If you get stuck you can find the answers on p61.

N	C	N	L	F	M	O	K	J	J	V	Z
Q	S	H	C	A	O	C	E	G	A	T	S
T	D	W	Z	Y	T	L	V	L	R	B	R
A	R	K	A	T	A	T	T	O	O	V	C
S	I	R	V	G	D	M	R	L	K	Y	P
T	M	A	R	V	G	N	Z	P	L	G	N
R	A	M	O	Z	C	E	I	Y	K	R	B
O	G	I	T	K	P	N	R	H	E	F	Z
R	I	R	C	X	K	E	J	V	H	T	V
R	N	P	A	G	H	X	L	H	D	C	N
W	E	D	F	C	Q	A	R	V	L	C	V
N	M	R	X	V	M	S	K	C	I	T	S

X FACTOR	ASTRO	PRIMARK
MALVERN	PINK	CHERYL
TATTOO	STICKS	STAGECOACH
SWAGGER	LEO	IMAGINE

we love you...

13

All About Cher

name: Cher Lloyd

BORN: JULY 28, 1993

place of birth: Malvern, Worcestershire

EYES: BROWN

height: 5'4"

STAR SIGN: LEO

family: Father Darren, mother Dina. One younger brother, Josh, and two younger sisters Sophie and Rosie.

RECORD LABEL: SYCO, EPIC RECORDS

DEBUT SINGLE: Swagger Jagger

CHER TRIVIA:

- *She had previously auditioned for The X Factor in 2008 but didn't get through the first round.*

- She has eight tattoos, including one of butterflies and birds.

- *The tattoo on her hand is of a musical note which is very similar to Cheryl Cole's.*

- If she could take just three things to a desert island she would choose her iPod, her Gran and her favourite food, pork pies.

- *She has, she says, a "love/hate relationship" with socks.*

- Her favourite restaurant is McDonalds.

v She has, she says, a "love/hate relationship" with socks

< Her favourite restaurant is McDonalds

15

X Factor Songlist

Cher 'smashed it' week after week on
The *X Factor*. Here is the full lowdown on
what she sang each week and reactions
from those who witnessed them first-hand!

FIRST AUDITION:
"Get Your Swag On",
by Soulja Boy
Cheryl Cole: "Cher - you
are right up my street! You're
actually, for me, my favourite
audition so far."

BOOT CAMP:
"Viva La Vida",
by Coldplay
Nicole Scherzinger: "I like
that she's original and unique
and she made it her own."

JUDGES' HOUSES:
"Cooler Than Me",
Mike Posner
Cheryl Cole: "I think she's got
'it', that's the frustrating thing.
She's only 16."

WEEK ONE:
"Just Be Good To Me",
The SOS Band.
Dannii Minogue: "Cher, I
absolutely loved that. You are
so watchable, I can't take my
eyes off you, you sounded
fantastic, you're a star."

WEEK TWO:
"It's A Hard Knock Life",
by Jay Z
Simon Cowell:
"I... absolutely... loved it! You
are exciting, you take risks,
you're interesting,
you're different."

WEEK THREE:
"No Diggity/Shout",
by Blackstreet/Tears
for Fears
Louis Walsh: "I loved what
you did on-stage. It was like you
were in your comfort zone. I love
your whole attitude."

WEEK FOUR:
"Stay",
by Shakespear's Sister
Cheryl Cole: "Honestly, you
did it babe. You put every single
emotion into it and we all felt it.
Here's the moment that the
nation gets to hear you sing.
It was epic, it was beautiful."

WEEK FIVE:
"Empire State of Mind",
by Jay-Z featuring Alicia Keys
Dannii Minogue: "It's like the song
could have been written for you. Really
loved it."

WEEK SIX:
"Sorry Seems to Be the
Hardest Word/Mockingbird",
by Elton John/Eminem
Simon Cowell: "I think after that,
you are 100 percent back in the
game. Loved it."

WEEK SEVEN:
"Imagine", by John Lennon
Cheryl Cole: "You have shown
versatility. The difference with you,
the originality with you is that you
sing, you rap, you dance."

WEEK EIGHT:
"Girlfriend/ Walk This Way",
by Avril Lavigne/Run DMC
Dannii Minogue: "This was my
favourite performance of yours. It was
unreal, it just made me think 'I want to
go to your concert.'"

WEEK NINE: "Nothin' on
You/Love the Way You Lie", by
B.o.B ft. Bruno Mars/Eminem
Cheryl Cole: "Your performance
does have a lot of attitude, which
is a part of you I absolutely love.
Backstage you're a 17-year-old
girl with a dream and fears like
everybody else."

WEEK TEN: "The Clapping
Song/ Get Ur Freak On",
by Shirley Ellis/Missy Elliott
Simon Cowell: "Cher, using one
of Cheryl's expressions, I'm going to
say that you 'smashed' that!"
**DUET: "Where Is The Love/I
Gotta Feeling", by Black Eyed
Peas (duet with will.i.am)
will.i.am:** "She reminds me of
when [we] started the group and
we were misfits, we didn't belong,
people thought we were odd. It takes
people like us that uniqueness can
be appreciated. This is a star."

17

Spotted!

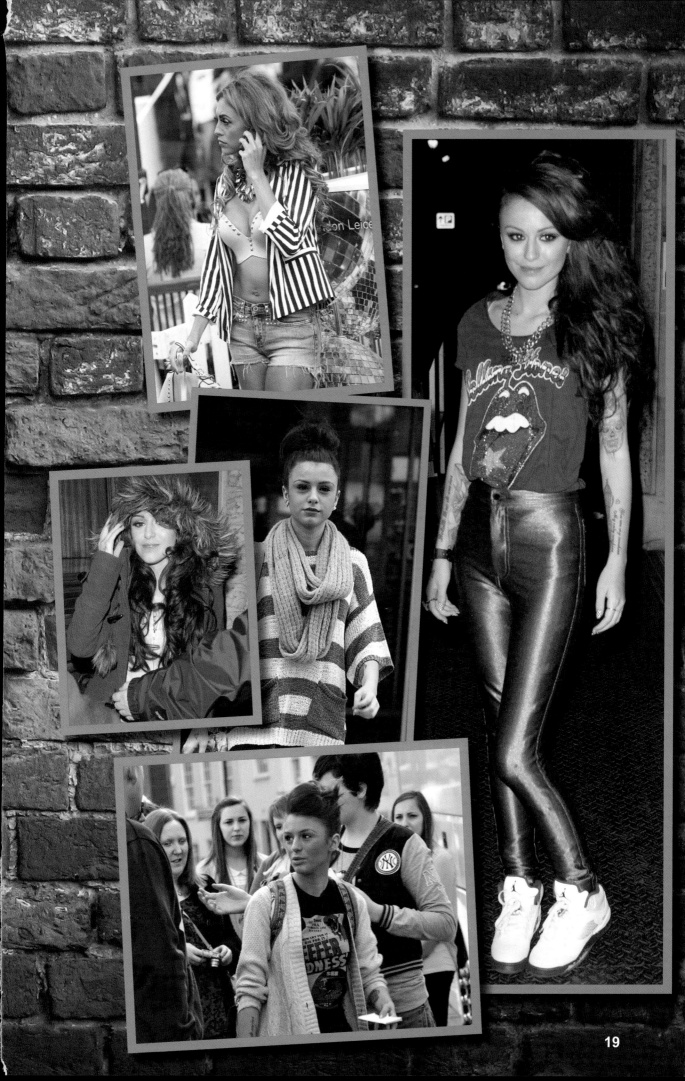

Cher's Famous

"I love Cher Lloyd"
will.i.am.

"She's a lovely young lady."
Aston of JLS

"I'm so proud of what [she] has achieved."
Cheryl Cole

"Yeah, I think Cher Lloyd's really cool - I love her songs."
Taio Cruz

"Cher was great... She's feisty, but I really liked her"
Dermot O'Leary

"She is pop perfection!"
Matt Cardle

"She sang a very contemporary song and I think that's always nice to hear."
Former Spice Girl, Emma Bunton, on Cher's *X Factor* audition

"Cher Lloyd is an incredible singer."
Mike Posner

"She has really brought something different and that's what we need."
Former *X Factor* winner, Shane Ward

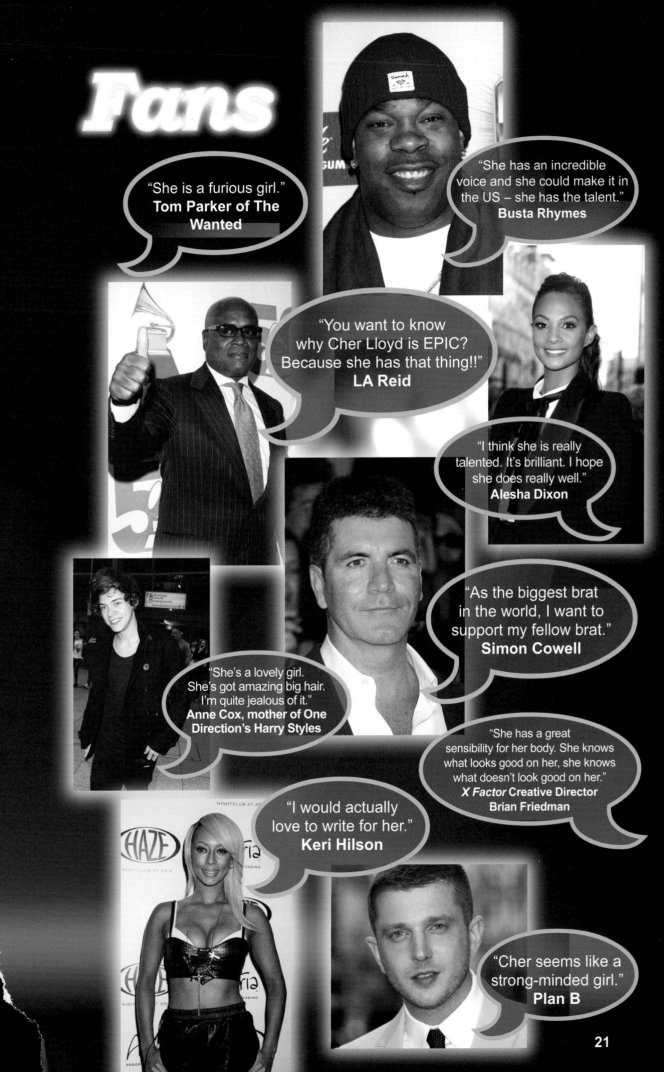

Fans

"She is a furious girl."
Tom Parker of The Wanted

"She has an incredible voice and she could make it in the US – she has the talent."
Busta Rhymes

"You want to know why Cher Lloyd is EPIC? Because she has that thing!!"
LA Reid

"I think she is really talented. It's brilliant. I hope she does really well."
Alesha Dixon

"As the biggest brat in the world, I want to support my fellow brat."
Simon Cowell

"She's a lovely girl. She's got amazing big hair. I'm quite jealous of it."
Anne Cox, mother of One Direction's Harry Styles

"She has a great sensibility for her body. She knows what looks good on her, she knows what doesn't look good on her."
X Factor Creative Director Brian Friedman

"I would actually love to write for her."
Keri Hilson

"Cher seems like a strong-minded girl."
Plan B

21

Life After The X Factor!

Since she graduated from Britain's biggest talent show in December 2010, life has been excitingly hectic for Cher. Here we bring you a month-by-month guide to what your favourite singer has been up to!

JANUARY 2011: Cher had little time to rest after her *X Factor* journey and was thrown into a hectic schedule of media appearances, negotiations and planning. She quickly learned what life was like as a famous figure - and she loved it.

FEBRUARY - APRIL 2011: Taking part in *The X Factor* Live Tour, Cher got a crash course in live performance. Around half a million people watched these concerts, meaning Cher had already sung in front of more people than most pop singers do in their entire careers!

MAY 2011: Work continued on her debut album. Cher became quite the expert in the recording studio as she quickly grasped how to sound brilliant on record.

JUNE 2011: Her first single, "Swagger Jagger", received its first airplay. Cher was so thrilled and proud to have her song on the airwaves!

JULY 2011: The aforementioned single was released at the end of the month. Cher could hardly believe it - a year ago she was an unknown and now her music was on sale in the shops! In the same month, several tracks from her forthcoming album were previewed. The fans loved them.

AUGUST 2011: Cher's debut single gets to number one in the UK charts. Cue ecstatic mayhem.

SEPTEMBER 2011: The pop industry moves fast and in this month her second single, "With Ur Love", was previewed on UK radio stations.

OCTOBER 2011: "With Ur Love" was released. Another hit for Cher!

NOVEMBER 2011: Her debut album, *Sticks + Stones* is unveiled. Not only that, Cher also announces her first tour, which will take place the following spring.

DECEMBER 2011: Already ruling the roost in the UK, Cher gets a boost to her American aspirations when LA Reid signs her to his Epic label. Totally awesome!

JANUARY 2012: "Want U Back" is released in the UK. A great start to the year for Cher.

FEBRUARY 2012: She speaks out against cyberbulling on BBC One's Panorama documentary. It was a brave and moving stance for her to adopt. Take that, bullies!

MARCH 2012: Never one to sit still, Cher begins planning and working on her second album. You can't keep a good girl down.

APRIL 2012: Her *Sticks + Stones* tour, which began at the end of the previous month, concludes triumphantly in London. Cher rocked big houses across the UK.

MAY 2012: Her American dream becomes reality as the pop princess wows American fans with her appearances, performances and general brilliance.

JUNE 2012: Her Stateside success saga continues apace. Cher is mobbed by fans outside radio stations. Alongside The Wanted and fellow *X Factor* graduates One Direction, she makes Americans sit up and take notice of British pop. Long may that - and Cher's success overall - continue.

we love you...

True or False?

1. Cher also auditioned for *Popstars: The Rivals*, the show that brought Cheryl Cole to fame!

2. She sang "Turn My Swag On" at her first *X Factor* audition.

3. Her first tour was called the "Ring-A-Ding" tour.

4. She was born in 1993.

5. Her mentor on *The X Factor* was Cheryl Cole.

6. Cher's favourite type of music is heavy metal.

7. LA Reid, who signed her to Epic Records, also signed pop superstar Justin Bieber.

8. Her boyfriend Craig Monk is a hairdresser.

9. Her debut single was called "Mick Jagger".

10. During her *X Factor* journey she was described as Dannii Minogue's 'mini-me'.

11. At bootcamp she sang "Wonderwall" by Oasis.

12. She grew up in Worcestershire.

13. Her father is called Derek.

14. She sang "Imagine" by John Lennon on *The X Factor*.

15. She once worked in a safari park in Iceland.

Answers on p61.

American Dream!

Cracking the American market is a tough task for any British pop act. For every success story such as One Direction, there are dozens of acts who fell at the first Yankee hurdle. You can follow Cher's exciting Stateside journey right here.

She approached the task full of confidence. "I'm off to smash open some doors in the US," she said as she left.

She added: "I want to do well out there. I've got big dreams. Even though I've achieved [success in the UK], there's so much more I want to do."

LA Reid, the judge on teh US version of the *X Factor* who also guided the careers of pop royalty such as Mariah Carey, Rihanna, Usher, Justin Bieber and Kanye West, signed her to his Epic label.

Reid introduced her at her showcase in New York, during which she thrilled fans with a seven-track set at the Canal Room. The set list included two covers: Robyn's "Dancing on My Own" and Usher's "OMG."

Her first conventional American concert appearance came at South by Southwest Music Conference and Festival in Austin, Texas. She got rave reviews for her performance.

As she embarked on her promotional tour of America, she unveiled a new look: a toned body and a shorter hairstyle. It went down a treat in the USA.

She has become a firm favourite of top American celebrity blogger, Perez Hilton. "We adore the former *X Factor* ferocity that is Cher Lloyd," he wrote.

The influential Billboard magazine loved her too and tipped her music to be 'a summer smash'.

She was mobbed by American fans as she left a radio station in Philadelphia. They ended up chasing her car down the street!

Cher was also besieged by fans in Florida. As she arrived at a radio station they mobbed her, with one fan falling onto her knees in front of her heroine!

There are rumours she will duet with stars including Mike Posner, Busta Rhymes and Snoop Dogg.

She has also enjoyed success in other foreign countries, including New Zealand where she had a Top 40 hit.

Spot the Difference

Cher looks gorgeous in this photograph of her signing copies of her CD, but there are 7 differences between these photos – how many can you spot?

Answers on p61.

Cher *Live!*

2. Cher performing at UEA Norwich, March 2012

3. Cher on stage at the E4 Stars of 2011 concert, Earls Court, London

1. Cher at the O2 Academy, Liverpool in April 2012

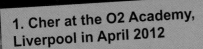

4. Cher at Party in the Park in Leeds, July 2011

6. Cher on the *X Factor* tour in Glasgow, April 2011

5. Cher at Key 103 Live, MEN Arena Manchester in July 2011

31

The A-Z of

A: **Astro** - The American rapper, who came to fame through *X Factor USA*, duetted with Cher on "Want U Back".

B: **Brats** - the affectionate term she uses to describe her fans

C: **Cheryl Cole** - Cher's relationship with the Girls Aloud star, who mentored her on the show, has been a rollercoaster

D: **Derriere** - Cher admits she has eaten kebabs in the hope of boosting her behind, saying: "I'd love to have a big a**e".

E: **Engagement** - Cher got engaged to Craig Monk in 2011

F: **Family** - "I hope one day we'll be... having kids."

G: **Grime** - One of her favourite musical genres is Grime!

H: **Hard work** - Cher has sweated hard to get her success, which she richly deserves!

I: **Internet** - Few celebrities have suffered more online negativity than Cher. "The internet's an evil thing," she said.

J: **Johnny Robinson** - She is a big fan of camp Johnny, who entertained the nation during the 2011 series of *X Factor*. "I love a bit of Johnny, me," she said.

K: **Knowledge** - Cher has had to learn fast about the highs and lows of fame - and she has done so!

L: **Lily Allen** - The famous, feisty Allen admires Cher and has stood up for her online.

M: **Modelling** - Having signed a deal with modelling agency Select, Cher is ready for the catwalk!

Cher Lloyd

N: Nicki Minaj - The rapper, singer/songwriter is one of Cher's favourite artists. "She's amazing," said Cher.

O: Originality - Cher rejects the idea that she is attempting to be anyone but herself. "I'm not copying anyone," she said.

P: Panorama - Tired of abuse from online bullies, Cher appeared on the BBC current affairs show to stand up against internet trolls.

Q: Quotes - Few modern pop stars are as outspoken and frank as Cher!

R: Runner-up - Far from being disappointed she didn't win *X Factor*, Cher believes she benefited from avoiding the pressure and expectation the winner gets. "It's a blessing," she said.

S: Swagger Jagger - her debut single which reached number one in the UK charts.

T: Tour - Cher's latest UK tour took in over 12 cities in April 2012.

U: United States of America - Cher feared failing in America but she has become quite a hit Stateside and loves life out there.

V: Vocalist - Cher's vocal talent has been celebrated by musical genius Mike Posner. "She is an incredible singer," he said.

W: With Ur Love - Her second single, released in the autumn of 2011, was a top-five hit in Britain!

X: X Factor - The show that brought Cher to the nation's attention!

Y: Younger siblings - She loves her little sisters and brother!

Z: Jay Z - Cher performed two of his tracks on *X Factor*. They are now buddies!

Dolly Parton

Cher has said she would "love" to collaborate with the country music legend. When she was growing up, Cher's parents would play Parton's songs in the house. Sometimes, Cher's dad would pop her up on the table and get her to sing along to the catchy tunes.

Heroes,
Influences and

Britney Spears

The brilliance of Britney has hit Cher more than once. The American superstar is a long-term influence on her. "I listened to her when I was growing up - yeah she's great," said Cher. She hopes to collaborate with Britney one day. That could be quite a tune.

Bashy, JME and Wiley

Underground and grime artists are among Cher's favourite acts. "I'm a big fan of Bashy," she said. Their influence on her musical sound, image and approach to life is clear. Cher hopes to incorporate more of this genre into her material in the future.

James Blake

She thinks that Dubstep singer James is a breath of fresh air in the UK music scene. "Proper inspiring," she said of him.

Fergie

Cher's debut album *Sticks + Stones* was compared to the Black Eyed Peas star's sound by its producer Savan Kotecha.

Just as Cher is a hero to so many, does the princess of pop admire anyone herself?

Inspirations

Emeli Sandé

A firm favourite of *X Factor* boss Simon Cowell, Emeli was named Brit Awards Critics' Choice for 2012. She has written music for Cher, who deeply admires her.

Nicki Minaj

Nicki is hardly short of fans at the moment - and Cher is very much one of them. "I just love the way that she works when she's on-stage, I just love her music and her style," said Cher. For one photo shoot, she rocked a two-tone hair colour with lips to match and looked most like Minaj!

Gwen Stefani

Another famous lady Cher has been influenced by in the style department is Gwen Stefani. She has worn a fluorescent bra with a translucent white vest that looked sensationally 'Stefaniesque'.

The Cher Lloyd Mega Quiz

Think you know all there is to know about Cher Lloyd? Then put yourself to the test with this testing trivia quiz.

1. What name does Cher use for her fans: brats or beauties?
2. Which band was Cher's *X Factor* mentor Cheryl Cole in?
3. What is Cher's father called?
4. Which county did Cher grow up in: Worcestershire or Berkshire?
5. What is the name of Cher's debut album?
6. And what was her debut single called?
7. Which star sign is Cher: Leo or Gemini?
8. Which record label is Cher signed to in America?
9. What was the name of Cher's first solo tour?
10. Which television channel is *X Factor* on?
11. What position did Cher finish in her series of *X Factor*?
12. And what year did she appear on the show?
13. How many siblings does Cher have?
14. Which song did Cher perform at judges' houses?
15. Which single saw Cher duet with Astro?
16. In which year did Cher release her debut single in the UK?
17. What is Cher's username on Twitter?
18. What is the name of the final track on *Sticks + Stones*?
19. And in which month in 2011 was it released?
20. What does 'Cher' mean in French?

Answers on p60.

The Tweets of Cher

Since opening her Twitter account (@CherLloyd), the pop princess has written thousands of 'Tweets' that give a charming insight into her day to day life. Here is a selection of her more entertaining messages...

"Gooooood morninggggg! Xxxxx"

"Hate it when nail varnish is just a big pile of gloop! Any wayyyy.... I hope everyone has a great day!!! Let me know what ur all up to!"

"Will I need some wellies for all this festival stuff? If it rains it could get muddy!! Haha x"

"Happy fathers day daddy!!!! I love u xxxx @dabbel2"

"Lasagne and chips, get in ma belly!!!!"

"In the warmth, got my jammas on watching telly! :) how's everyones day been?"

"hope everyone had a great christmas ! roll on new year! xxx"

"I didn't used to like salads."

"Damnnn, I don't like it when I see pictures that I didn't know were taken, sneeeaky! God job I wasn't pickin my nose or anythin ;) hahaa!"

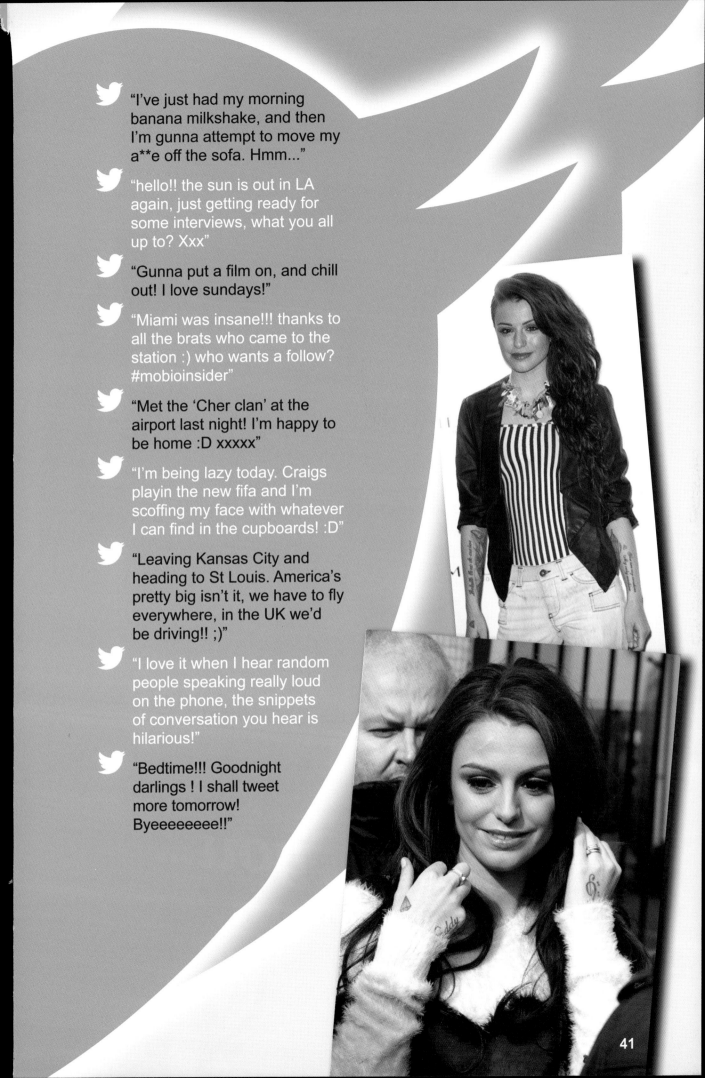

"I've just had my morning banana milkshake, and then I'm gunna attempt to move my a**e off the sofa. Hmm..."

"hello!! the sun is out in LA again, just getting ready for some interviews, what you all up to? Xxx"

"Gunna put a film on, and chill out! I love sundays!"

"Miami was insane!!! thanks to all the brats who came to the station :) who wants a follow? #mobioinsider"

"Met the 'Cher clan' at the airport last night! I'm happy to be home :D xxxxx"

"I'm being lazy today. Craigs playin the new fifa and I'm scoffing my face with whatever I can find in the cupboards! :D"

"Leaving Kansas City and heading to St Louis. America's pretty big isn't it, we have to fly everywhere, in the UK we'd be driving!! ;)"

"I love it when I hear random people speaking really loud on the phone, the snippets of conversation you hear is hilarious!"

"Bedtime!!! Goodnight darlings ! I shall tweet more tomorrow! Byeeeeeeee!!"

we love you...

42

we love you...

Who is Astro?

He duetted with Cher on her single "Want U Back".
But just who is Astro?

Like Cher, Astro came to fame
through *X Factor* - but in his case it
was the American version. He says
he had been making music 'since
he was a baby' but started doing it
seriously when he turned 10.

The boy from Brooklyn auditioned
on the first series of *X Factor USA*.
He might have been just 15 years
old at the time, but Astro made
quite an impact. He performed a
self-written song entitled "Stop
Lookin' At My Mom." It is always
a risk to sing an unfamiliar song
at an audition but he quickly
had the entire audience dancing
and singing along to the
infectious song.

He sailed through to the live shows
and became a controversial figure
once he got to them. While his
performances were superb, his
attitude was called into question
by the judges when he reacted
badly to being voted into the
bottom two. He was eventually
voted out and finished seventh.

After the series ended, Astro
continued to be one of its most
memorable figures. He was signed
by LA Reid to the Epic label. "It's
like a dream," said Astro as he
inked his deal. Reid, who had also
signed Cher to his label, quickly
decided to pair them up on "Want U
Back". The result was magnificent!

WOOD *summer!*

Afterwards, she Tweeted the show's judges - including Sharon Osbourne - to thank them: '@ MrsSOsbourne @ HowardStern @ HowieMandel @ NickCannon and the crew of AGT, I'd like to say thank you so much for having me! Really enjoyed it!'

One day in Hollywood, she helped make drinks at a milk shake outlet. So many of her fans turned up for a chance to get a milk shake made by their hero that police had to close the venue. Over 3,000 'Brats' turned up!

She came 25th in FHM's 100 sexiest women list.

Cher's Causes...

Since becoming a celebrity, Cher has used her fame to help promote worthy causes. Whether donating signed goodies, performing at fundraising concerts, answering phones at fundraising centres or just speaking out, she has proved quite the champion of causes.

Cyberbullying

The issue that Cher is most associated with is the fight against online bullying. She has spoken out about this problem several times, most notably on the BBC One documentary series *Panorama*. Having faced an avalanche of online abuse herself, she knows better than most how nasty it is.

Cher said that she regularly cries herself to sleep because of nasty things that 'online trolls' have said to her. "I must get at least ten tweets a day saying I'm a dirty pikey," she told the programme. "I think they know it's going to get to me, or because they know they can."

She called for the government to do more to tackle online bullying and she also encouraged young people who are suffering from cyber abuse to seek support from their friends. "I never thought I could talk to anybody about it because I didn't feel I needed to as I was strong enough to get through it alone, but that's the worst thing you can do," she said.

Other issues and ventures

In November 2010, Cher and her fellow *X Factor* finalists released a cover of the David Bowie hit "Heroes". It sold 144,000 copies in its first week, and went straight to number one, with all the proceeds going to the Help For Heroes charity.

In October 2011, she supported Capital FM's Help A Capital Child Appeal. Wearing a more demure outfit than usual, she helped answer phones at the Appeal's headquarters.

The following month, big-hearted Cher donated one of her coats to Daybreak's Donate a Coat appeal. The appeal used the funds to help needy young mothers and their families in the Leeds area.

She had previously donated signed items to the Oh! What A Night fundraiser in Coventry, which raised money for the Alzheimer's Society.

In July 2012, she performed at the MFEST festival at Harewood House, in aid of the Morrisons charity, Raise a Smile.

She also appeared at the Tartan Gig 2012 which helped raise funds for the Girl Guides.

"I have always been quite a big Britney fan."

"I don't do things by half-measure. It's got to be perfect."

"I always wanted to rap but never really had the guts to do it because I'm just a skinny white girl. Then aged 13 I started rapping secretly because I didn't know whether people would accept me — some people still don't."

"I love food.. but let's just say I'm not overly adventurous! I'm trying though... really I am! As long as I've got my chips on the side... then I'll try something new."

"People don't want to see me going through the puppet machine again, they want to see me as an artist."

"People will never know the meaning of some songs because they're too personal to explain, but if they like me and the song so much, they should know what it's about. I prefer it when people have different interpretations of the song and use their imagination."

"He's been great - absolutely brilliant actually. He treats me like a star and he's really, really nice. He also eats a lot of scrambled egg!" (On L.A. Reid.)

Cher Says...

Ms Lloyd has always got plenty to say. Here are some particularly memorable moments of wit, wisdom and weirdness...

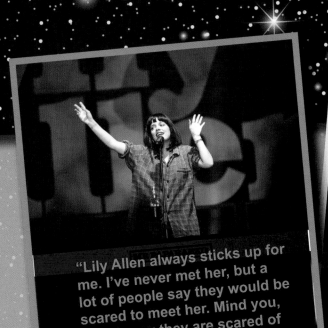

"Lily Allen always sticks up for me. I've never met her, but a lot of people say they would be scared to meet her. Mind you, people say they are scared of meeting me too."

"I didn't listen to Girls Aloud growing up, no way," she says scornfully. "Too cheesy, man! I listened to grime, garage, bashment."

"I used to think being a pop star would be glamorous, but it's not. Some days are good and some are bad. I'm happy though because it's got me where I am today."

"I'd rather wear Primark than Prada. I'd rather spend my money making my family happy."

"I'm not doing all this hard work for nothing! At the end of the day it's for my career, it's not for anyone else."

"D'you know what? A lot of things have been said about me. People are going to talk and that's a good thing; I want people to talk."

"I'm two completely different people. Backstage I am a nervous wreck, I'm actually nearly crying. And then as soon as my foot goes on the stage, that's it, I'm a different person."

we love you...

Cher Crossword

Across

2   Cher's favourite vegetable (7)

5   The name of the town Cher grew up in (7)

6   What Cher loves doing more than anything (7)

7   Cher's mentor on *X Factor* was _____ Cole (6)

8   LA Reid signed Cher to his ____ label in America (4)

9   The month Cher was born (4)

10 The affectionate nickname Cher has given to her fans (5)

13 The boy band who finished one place above Cher on *X Factor* is One _____ (9)

Down

1   The head judge in Cher's *X Factor* year is _____ Cowell (5)

3   The BBC documentary series she appeared on (8)

4   The winner in Cher's *X Factor* year was Matt _____ (6)

5   Cher's favourite animal. Cheeky! (6)

6   Cher's debut album is called _____ & Stones (6)

9   Her debut single was called Swagger _____ (6)

11 Her UK record label (4)

12 The name of the American rapper who appeared on "Want U Back" (5)

Answers on p60.

we *love* you...

we love you...

55

Cher loves...

Find out right here what gets Cher buzzing in life, in this collection of her very favourite things!

ANIMAL: Monkeys

TV SHOW: Eastenders

KIDS' TV SHOW: Blue Peter

SNACKS: Spicy flavoured crisps

DRINKS: Dr Pepper

FAVOURITE COLOUR: Baby pink

FOOD: Chinese - "I'd eat it every single day if I could."

VEGETABLE: Parsnips

POP GUILTY PLEASURE: Steps - "I love a bit of 'Tragedy'. I really enjoy them!"

FILM: Hocus Pocus

GIRL CRUSHES: Nicki Minaj, Katy Perry, Jessie J, Beyoncé and Kat Von D.

WEBSITES: YouTube and various R&B blogs - she uses both to spot up-and-coming singers!

CARTOON CHARACTER: SpongeBob Squarepants

COSMETICS: Iman bronzer

SHOPS: Topshop and Urban Outfitters

The Successometer!

Follow Cher's career as she gets hotter and hotter!

April 2012:
She hits the USA, where she embarks on a hectic and successful promotional tour!

March 2012:
Cher's debut tour kicks off in Folkestone. The sell-out tour concludes in London the following month by which time it had been seen by nearly 30,000 people.

February 2012:
Her third single, "Want U Back", is released, handing Cher her second UK number one.

December 2011:
Cher signs a deal with American label Epic after impressing the legendary LA Reid.

November 2011:
Her album *Sticks + Stones* is released.

August 2011:
Her debut single, "Swagger Jagger", gets to number one in the UK chart!

February 2011:
Cher joins the *X Factor* live tour, which sees her perform in front of half a million delighted fans during its three-month run!

December 2010:
...and makes it all the way to the final in December, finishing in fourth place. Simon Cowell immediately signs her to SyCo.

October 2010:
Cher joins the live shows of *X Factor*, facing the public vote each week....

July 2010:
Gets through boot camp at Wembley Arena and attends the judges' houses phase in Ascot, Berkshire, where she sings to Cheryl Cole and will.i.am!

June 2010:
Cher auditions for *X Factor*, singing "Get Your Swag On".

Quiz answers

The Cher Lloyd Mega Quiz Page 38

1. Brats
2. Girls Aloud
3. Darren
4. Worcestershire
5. Sticks + Stones
6. Swagger Jagger
7. Leo
8. Epic
9. The Sticks + Stones Tour
10. ITV
11. Fourth
12. 2010
13. Three
14. Cooler Than Me
15. Want U Back
16. 2011
17. @CherLloyd
18. End Up Here
19. November
20. 'Dear'

Crossword
Page 53

Crossword grid answers:

- 2 Across: PARSNIP
- 5 Across: MALVERN
- 6 Across: SINGING
- 7 Across: CHERYL
- 8 Across: EPIC
- 9 Across: JULY
- 10 Across: BRATS
- 13 Across: DIRECTION
- 1 Down: SIMONO
- 2 Down: MONKEY
- 3 Down: PARNOROAM
- 4 Down: CARDLEE
- 6 Down: STICKS
- 7 Down: CHERYLAM
- 9 Down: JAGGE
- 11 Down: SYCO
- 12 Down: ASTR

True or False?
Page 26

1 False
2 True
3 False
4 True
5 True
6 False
7 True
8 True
9 False
10 False
11 False
12 True
13 False
14 True
15 False

Spot the difference
Page 30

Wordsearch
Page 12

N	C	N	L	F	M	O	K	J	J	V	Z
Q	S	H	C	A	O	C	E	G	A	T	S
T	D	W	Z	Y	T	L	V	L	R	B	R
A	R	K	A	T	A	T	T	O	O	V	C
S	I	R	V	G	D	M	R	L	K	Y	P
T	M	A	R	V	G	N	Z	P	L	G	N
R	A	M	O	Z	C	E	I	Y	K	R	B
O	G	I	T	K	P	N	R	H	E	F	Z
R	I	R	C	X	K	E	J	V	H	T	V
R	N	P	A	G	H	X	L	H	D	C	N
W	E	D	F	C	Q	A	R	V	L	C	V
N	M	R	X	V	M	S	K	C	I	T	S

Where's Cher?